Lara, Forever

Youssef Khalim

Copyright © 2013 Youssef Khalim

All rights reserved.

ISBN: 978-0-9787810-3-3
ISBN-13: 978-0978781033

DEDICATION

To: Larisa (The real or ideal soul mate: inspiration)

       Tonya Tracy Khalim and

       Runako Soyini Khalim, (my most beloved daughters)

       Mother and Grandmother and Great-grandmother, (my most beloved maternal biological ancestors, and spiritual antecedents)

       M. A. Garvey (one of my 7 M's: my role models)

       Youssef Khalim II; III (my most beloved sons)

       Father and Grandfather and Great-grandfather, (my most beloved paternal biological ancestors, and spiritual antecedents).

To: The Forerunners and Reincarnation sources (beloved biological ancestors and spiritual antecedents), and

       The Almighty (our Spiritual Father), from whence we come.

CONTENTS

	Acknowledgments	i
1	Introduction	1
2	My Dream Come True	Pg 2
3	Re: Carry Outs	Pg 4
4	When I See You Baby	Pg 5
5	Extraordinary Beauty	Pg 6
6	Thanks	Pg 8
7	Let Me Experience	Pg 9
8	I Love to See You Pose	Pg 11
9	Signs I'm Falling In Love With You	Pg 12
10	All I Want For Christmas Is You	Pg 14
11	Golden Girl	Pg 16
12	Any Man Will Fall In Love With You	Pg 18
13	You Too Will Love Heaven	Pg 19
14	I Love To See Your Body Move	Pg 20
15	Sacred Site	Pg 21
16	I have To Have You	Pg 22
17	I Bet You Will Love Me Too	Pg 23
18	Friendship	Pg 25
19	I Can't Get You Outta My Mind	Pg 26
20	I Will Do Anything For You	Pg 27
21	Love: To The Whole Wide World	Pg 28
22	About The Author, And Other Books	Pg 29

ACKNOWLEDGMENTS

To: The Forerunners and Reincarnation sources (beloved biological ancestors and spiritual antecedents), and

The Almighty (our Spiritual Father), from whence we come.

Natasha - Photography

1 INTRODUCTION

Lara, Forever is the first in a series of eight books by Youssef Khalim, begun in 2002. Four were inspired by ladies encountered overseas. *Lara* is one of the four inspired by Americans.

Khalim says, "I met Lara in the summer of 2001, at a real-life Cheers-like, Cocktail Lounge and Bar, where she bartends. I remember our first meeting because you can't forget her eyes. And I was writing *for* her from the very beginning because I had to write down the words, "Rhine Wine," to make her understand what I wanted.

"Later, I was struck by her extraordinary beauty and lovely personality. I wrote down feelings and experiences to form this book.

"In the fall of 2001, she went to Las Vegas, and she was gone for about a week. I missed her so much that I composed *You Too Will Love Heaven*, upon her return. With the creative juices now flowing, I completed *Extraordinary Beauty*. Then, I was inspired to do *Golden Girl*, and later, *Signs I'm Falling In Love With You*, by Lara, and one of our mutual friends.

"All of this writing was going on around Christmas time, 2001. So, it was a lot of fun to do *All I Want For Christmas Is You*. Lara has the most beautiful body, and walk. So, I suggested to her that she would make an ideal model - not knowing that she had already been doing modeling. Her modeling and body-beautiful is reflected in selections completed around the New Year of 2002. I completed *I Love To See Your Body Move, Any Man Will Fall In Love With You*, and *When I See You Baby*. I had great fun composing *When I See You Baby* and *Re: Carry Outs*. In January, 2002, I completed the last poem of that series, *I Love To See You Pose*.

"When the writing started again, in March, I completed *Re: Carry Outs*, and *Let Me Experience*. Then came *My Dream Come True, Thanks, Sacred Site*, and *Love: To The Whole Wide World*. At this time I realized that we had a whole book, essentially in tribute to the beauty and personality of one woman-a first for me. It was very easy to complete *I Have To Have You*, and *Friendship*. It was great fun adding the graphics to *I Bet You Will Love Me Too*."

And now I present to you the exciting, electric, and exotic *Lara, Forever*. Enjoy.

                                        Youssef Khalim
                                        6/19/02

2 MY DREAM COME TRUE

I wish I could say
How much I love you:

Touch your hand,
And touch your heart,

I wish I could hold you near,
And kiss you,

And I know that dreams come true.

I wish I could travel throughout the universe with you:

And bless you,
With the help of Heaven,

I wish I could hold you
In
My arms tonight,

And give you
What you need,

'Cause I know that dreams come true.

I wish to bless you,
Once again,

And wish to say
How much I love you,

I wish to
Restore
You to your Royal Place,

I want to see you live
Forever,

Have Heaven bless you, Yet again,

I promise,
I will always love you,
Because you are
My dream
Come true.

3 RE: CARRY OUTS

You have beautiful,
Sexy,
Gorgeous buns:

Frank(ly),
I'll take you:
Here, to go, or whatever,
With everything
Off.

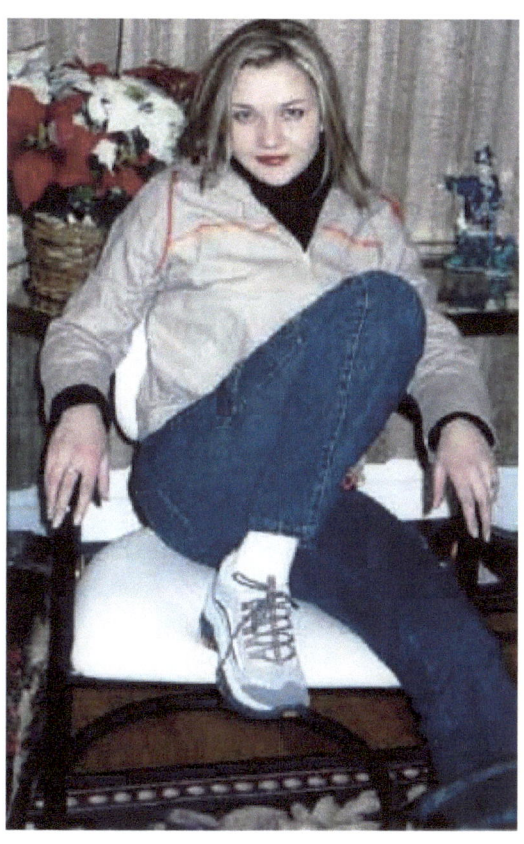

4 WHEN I SEE YOU BABY

When I see you baby,
My heart leaps for joy,

Hormones go crazy,
Vision hazy,
Like a boy with a brand new toy.

When I see you baby,
Your smile lights up my face,

And your Hot Body
Heats me up,
'Til I'm hot-to-go
For days.

Whenever I see you baby,
I want to see you,
All
Over
Again.

I have to see you,
See you,
See you,
See you,
And see you,
All over Again.

5 EXTRAORDINARY BEAUTY

You are The Extraordinary Beauty:

With your
Lovely,
Radiant smile,
And intoxicating eyes.

The way you walk is unbelievable:

And beyond
Gorgeous and
Sexy,
It's extraordinary.

You're pure inspiration:

Heaven on earth,
Divine,
Oceans of love and warmth,
Wonderful,
Sublime,
Powerful, grande, and majestic.

Your loving ways are:
Sweet, and kind, and generous.

To *behold* you is not enough.

I must hold you,

Know you

Adore you,

Touch you, taste you,

Please and serve you,
And love you totally,
Ever more.

My love for you will last forever,
I'll love you through the great hereafter,

I'll love you 'til all love
Throughout the universe becomes:

One precious gem of
Extraordinary beauty.

6 THANKS

Thanks for your
Gorgeous, wondrous
Presence, and

Heavenly
Inspiration.

I adore you.
I love you.

Me

7 LET ME EXPERIENCE

Let me experience
The full force
Of your female energy
Again:

Not just seeing
Your beautiful
And perfect:

Eyes,
Mouth,
Chest, &
Hips,

Butt, the sound of
Your voice;

To hear you whisper
The sound of bliss,

To feel your warm-hot, velvet body,
And taste your sweet,
Intoxicating
Mouth,

To feel the urgency of
Your body,

Finally,
Urging me on,
To feel

And experience
The full force
Of your female energy
Again.

8 I LOVE TO SEE YOU POSE

I love to watch your artful ways,
I love to see you
Pose:

Moving to the music

Rearranging your hair-then posing

Walking Smiling
Laughing Talking
Playing Friendly
Putting on lipstick
Lovely   Aglow
Sexy

Threatening to spray water on your friend,
Posing.

You are stunningly beautiful,
And
What you do

Naturally,

I love to see:

You
Pose.

9 SIGNS I'M FALLING IN LOVE WITH YOU

I want you Morning,
Noon,
And night,

I'm still amazed:
You have *the* most beautiful mouth
In the whole-wide world,

Your body
Excites me to no end,

You are gorgeous,
Sitting, standing, walking,
Or working;
And glamorous,
In jeans,

I adore you,
And when I see or think of you,
I *feel* bliss,

My soul sends you
Quiet and peaceful
Streams, beams, and gusts of
"I love you,"

I feel your presence in my heart,
And as part of my
Physical and
Spiritual self;
I see and hear you
In my dreams,

I love your mind,
And long for conversation
With you,

I want to live with you
A million years,

And, unlike this poem,
There is no end
To how much I love you.

10 ALL I WANT FOR CHRISTMAS IS YOU

I don't need no Christmas Tree,
To warm me for the season.

I just need you close to me,
To give you what you need.

I don't want a mistletoe
Unless you're underneath it.

I don't need no Jingle Bells,
Nor visit from Saint Nick.

I don't need your Christmas song,
With its catchy beat.

I just need you, baby
Right here next to me.

And all I want for Christmas,
All I need for Christmas,
All I want for Christmas,
Is ... you.

I don't need a lot of gifts,
Piled high beneath the tree.

Baby, let me tell you,
It's you I need to see.

I don't need no Yuletide feast,
To feed me, Christmas Day,

I don't need a football game,
If you come out to play.

And all I want for Christmas,
All I need for Christmas,
All I need for Christmas,
Is... you.

I don't need white, misty snow,
Reindeer can fly on by.

I get my lift when I'm with you,
Just looking in your eyes.

You're all I ever want (my love),
All I ever need,
And all I want for Christmas
Is… you.

11 GOLDEN GIRL

If I could give up all my wishes but just one,

I want to
Touch you,
Kiss you,

Taste the awesome beauty of your mouth,

Inhale your warmth and sweetness,
Feel your softness,

Make you feel like you're in heaven,
Fulfill your fantasies,

Plant angel kisses on your face,
Serve you joy and pleasure,

Celebrate your beauty,

Look deep into your lovely eyes,

Adore you,
Love you more each day,

Give you a gift each day
To make you smile,

Enjoy your friendly, sweet, engaging words,

Make you a bed of roses,

And love

Every inch

Of your

Tall and sexy,
Golden, gorgeous, body,

Then, love you,
And love you,
And love you all over again.

12 ANY MAN WILL FALL IN LOVE WITH YOU

Any man will fall in love with you,

When he sees the way you walk:

If he has a heart
And if he has a soul,

If he has the breath of life,
And if this man is whole.

Any man will fall in love with you,
When he *listens* to you,

Has a mind,
And thinks;

And if he listens to his heart,
And mind and heart are linked.

Any man will fall in love with you,
Since seasons come and go,
There is a universe,
And you are lovely,

And I am
Any man.

13 YOU TOO WILL LOVE HEAVEN

You are like
Heaven,

With your subtle,
Shocking,
Magnificent,
Intoxicating,
Beauty, and Power.

When I see you,

And scrape myself up off the floor,
(And gather myself together),

I can only say to those who do not know you:
"When you see her
You too will love heaven,"
Just as much as
I do.

14 I LOVE TO SEE YOUR BODY MOVE

You have the: Sexy,
Beautiful, Lovely,
Light, and
Graceful,
Perfect body.

And when you walk,
I love to see your body move.

When your body moves,
You have the most beautiful walk
In the whole, wide world.

I need to see you,
'Cause I love you;

Need to love you,
'Cause I love your gorgeous body;

I need to taste, and touch, and feel
Your:
Warm, sweet, sexy body,
As you move.

15 SACRED SITE

Your Beauty is
Sacred,

AWESOME,

Divine and Holy

In its sheer
Beauty.

16 I HAVE TO HAVE YOU

I could live without you
Until I met you.

But since I've met you,
I have to have you.
So, we'll do it your way.

Since I've got to have you,
I'll take you any way you want it.

Any time,
Anywhere,

Let me take you:
There.

17 I BET YOU WILL LOVE ME TOO

I love you so much
That I bet
There will come a day,
And you will love me too.

I know you're looking for true love,
'Cause time has taken you to that door.

And as you move to open up,
Life will bless you even more,

You look so ready,
'Cause whenever I see you, you look so fine,
I love to sip you, like you sip fine wine.

And, now that love is here to stay:
Can you take one kiss & walk away?

Can we spend one night together,
And forget about that day?

Can you come (in) close?
Would you rather go, or stay?

Now, they said there'd come a time,
When love would gush forth,
From every soul,

And the world would come around,
And you would love so much,
That you'd love everybody:

And say,
"I love you:"

Give it,
Want it,
Need it,
Feel it,
Taste it,
Breathe it,
Be it.

And on that day, (today),

I bet ya,
You will love me too.

18 FRIENDSHIP

Love may come and go
But friendship never ends.

So, first I want you
For my friend.

Then, you are my lover,
'Cause I need your body so bad.

Then, you are the mother
 Of our children,

Because we have become:

One soul

Under God

Indivisible

With liberty, justice, and joy

For all.

19 I CAN'T GET YOU OUTTA MY MIND

I think about you all the time.

I think about your hips,
And then, begin to trip!

I think about your face,
You put me in a daze!

I think about your walk,
I wanna talk with you.

I think about your eyes,
And then I'm mesmerized!

I wanna be with you,
Take a trip with you.

I wanna touch you, hold you, kiss you, love you,
'Till I can get you outta my mind!

20 I WILL DO ANYTHING FOR YOU

Yes, I will do anything.
Everything and anything.

I will do anything, for you.
I will do whatever.

I will do all-ever,
Then, I will do the next thing!
Anything and everything,

All the things that need some doing,
I will do them all!

Let's face it:
Whatever - must be done!
I will do it!

'Cause, I will do anything,
I will do whatever,

I will do anything,
For you.

OK, this is my bottom line:
I will do anything,
Yes, I will do anything,
To have you, hold you, keep you, squeeze you,
And then, I'll do the next thing,
Just for you,

And prove to you both day and night,
By making sure all things are right,

Then, love you with a love so strong,
It erases night; ergo be gone!

And show you, Baby, I will do anything,
For you!

21 LOVE: TO THE WHOLE WIDE WORLD

Loving you

Opened the

Floodgates of

Love:

To the

Whole
Wide
World.

22 ABOUT THE AUTHOR, AND OTHER BOOKS

Youssef Khalim obtained Unity in yoga on about 7/20/80. He says, "We will recombine into one faith, Judaism, Christianity, and Islam." He has been able to "see" and experience some amazing information about USA presidents Jefferson, Lincoln, and Obama; and also Prophets Moses, Muhammad, and Solomon - in visions, lucid dreams, and in meditation. Khalim makes reincarnation (resurrection) central again in our western religions. He resides in the Chicagoland area. And he is the father of Tonya, Runako, and Noah. See his books on the following websites: http://lulu.com and http://sunracommunications.com

OTHER BOOKS

Youssef Khalim's books include *People Of The Future/Day; You Are Too Beautiful; I Love You Back; You Look So Good; The Resurrection Of Noah; Healing Begins With The Mind; Jubilee Worldwide; Lara,* **Forever***; Tanisha Love; Galina, All About Love; Ekaterina, Hot and Lovely; Natalia, With Love; Svetlana, Angel Of Love; Lori, My Dream Girl*; *I Call My Sugar, Candie*; *Love of My Life*; and *The Second Coming!*

www.ingramcontent.com/pod-product-compliance
Lightning Source LLC
Chambersburg PA
CBHW040925190426
43197CB00032B/37